Sport and My Body

Cycling

Charlotte Guillain

Raintree

www.raintreepublishers.co.uk
Visit our website to find out more information about Raintree books.

To order:

☎ Phone +44 (0) 1865 888066

▤ Fax +44 (0) 1865 314091

▣ Visit www.raintreepublishers.co.uk

Raintree is an imprint of Capstone Global Library Limited, a company incorporated in England and Wales having its registered office at 7 Pilgrim Street, London, EC4V 6LB – Registered company number: 6695582

"Raintree" is a registered trademark of Pearson Education Limited, under licence to Capstone Global Library Limited

Edited by Siân Smith, Rebecca Rissman, and Charlotte Guillain
Designed by Joanna Hinton-Malivoire
Picture research by Ruth Blair
Production by Duncan Gilbert
Originated by Raintree
Printed and bound in China by South China Printing Company Ltd

ISBN 978 1 406 21114 6
13 12 11 10 09
10 9 8 7 6 5 4 3 2 1

British Library Cataloguing in Publication Data
Guillain, Charlotte.
 Cycling. -- (Sport and my body)
  1. Cycling--Physiological aspects--Juvenile literature.
  2. Cycling--Social aspects--Juvenile literature.
  I. Title II. Series
  613.7'11-dc22

Acknowledgements
We would like to thank the following for permission to reproduce photographs: Alamy pp.**11** (© Jenny Matthews), **17** (© Seb Rogers); Corbis pp.**5** (Wolfgang Rattay/Reuters), **10** (Sean Justice), **13** (Hill Street Studios/Stock This Way), **16** (Ariel Skelley), **21** (moodboard); Getty Images p.**15** (David McNew); iStockphoto pp.**18**, **22**, **20** (© Pathathai Chungyam), **22** (© David H. Lewis), **22** (© Craig Barhorst), **22** (© Michal Kolosowski); Photolibrary pp. **6**, **7**, **8**, **9**, **12**, **14**, **19**, **23**, **23**, **23**, **23**, **23**, **23**; Photoshot p.**4** (Liang Qiang/Xinhua).

Cover photograph of boys riding bicycles reproduced with permission of Getty Images/Sean Murphy/Lifesize. Back cover images reproduced with permission of iStockphoto: 1. bicycle pump (© Michal Kolosowski); 2. helmet (© David H. Lewis).

Every effort has been made to contact copyright holders of material reproduced in this book. Any omissions will be rectified in subsequent printings if notice is given to the publishers.

Contents

Some words are shown in bold, **like this**. You can find them in the glossary on page 23.

What is cycling?

When we ride a bicycle we are cycling.
Cycling is a type of exercise.

People cycle for sport or to get
to places. We can also cycle for fun.

How do I learn to cycle?

stabiliser

Many people learn to ride a bicycle with **stabilisers**. They help you to **balance** as you learn to ride.

When you are ready, you can take away the stabilisers. Then you learn to balance and **pedal** at the same time.

How do I use my legs and feet?

You use your legs to hold the bicycle still on the ground. To start moving you put one foot on the ground and push a **pedal** forwards with the other foot.

You use your legs and feet to pedal and move the bicycle. You can pedal fast or slowly.

How do I use my arms and hands?

brake

You use your hands to hold the handlebars and steer the bicycle. You might use your hands to ring a bell or use the **brakes**.

You can use your arms to show other people where you are going.

What happens to my body when I cycle?

When you cycle your heart starts to beat faster. You may feel hot and sweaty.

leg muscle

When you cycle fast you will breathe more quickly. The **muscles** in your legs will start to feel tired.

Why do we cycle?

When you cycle you can travel further and faster than when you walk. You can visit new places.

It is fun to cycle with friends. Everyone can learn to cycle.

How do I stay safe cycling?

A teacher can tell you how to cycle safely. It is important to wear a helmet when you are cycling.

If you are cycling in the evening, always use lights. You should also wear light-coloured clothes that drivers can see easily.

How do I look after my bicycle?

Keep your bicycle out of the rain when you are not using it. You might use a cycle lock to keep it safe.

tyre

Make sure your **brakes** are working properly. Always check your **tyres** are pumped up.

Does cycling make me healthy?

Cycling is good exercise and will help to keep you fit. You should also eat healthy food and drink plenty of water.

To stay healthy you need to get plenty of sleep. Then you can have fun in many different ways.

Cycling equipment

helmet

light

lock

pump

Glossary

 **balance** to keep yourself or an object steady so that it does not fall

 **brakes** you use the brakes on a bicycle to slow it down or stop it from moving

 **muscle** part of your body that helps you to move. Exercise can make muscles bigger and stronger.

 **pedal** part of a bicycle that you push on with your foot to make the bicycle move. When you use pedals to make something move this is called pedalling.

 **stabilisers** two extra wheels attached either side of a bicycle to make it balanced or steady

 **tyre** a thick rubber ring that covers the edge of a wheel. Tyres are usually filled with air.

Index

Find out more

http://www.direct.gov.uk/en/TravelAndTransport/
CyclingAndWalking/DG–10026401
This website has some great safety tips.

http://kidshealth.org/kid/watch/out/bike–safety.html
On this website, you can learn which hand signals you
should use when cycling.